This book belongs to:

_____

_____

_____

First published 2001 by Walker Books Ltd
87 Vauxhall Walk, London SE11 5HJ

This edition published 2011

2 4 6 8 10 9 7 5 3 1

"Maisy" Audio Visual Series produced by King Rollo Films for
Universal Pictures International Visual Programming

Maisy™. Maisy is a registered trademark of Walker Books Ltd, London.

Printed in China

British Library Cataloguing in Publication Data:
a catalogue record for this book is available from the British Library

ISBN 978-1-4063-3473-9

www.walker.co.uk
www.maisyfun.co.uk

Maisy Makes
Lemonade

Lucy Cousins

WALKER BOOKS
AND SUBSIDIARIES
LONDON · BOSTON · SYDNEY · AUCKLAND

Maisy is out in the sunshine today.

Mmmm, she's drinking delicious lemonade.

Hello, Eddie,
are you thirsty?

Sit down and have
some lemonade.

Eddie's still thirsty.

But, oh dear,
the lemonade has
all gone!

Maisy has an idea.

She goes to
the lemon tree in
the garden . . .

and she picks lots of lemons.

Thanks for the lift, Eddie!

In the kitchen
Eddie squeezes the
lemons into a jug.

Then Maisy adds
some water ...

and Eddie stirs in
the sugar.

Hooray!
A jug full of delicious
lemonade!

Maisy fetches some glasses.

Slurp, slurp!

Whatever is that noise, Maisy?

Oh, it's you, Eddie!
What delicious lemonade.

Now you'll have to
make some more!

Read and enjoy the Maisy story books

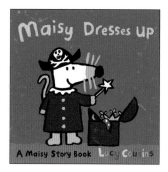

Maisy Dresses Up

A Maisy Story Book Lucy Cousins

Maisy's Bedtime

A Maisy Story Book Lucy Cousins

Maisy's Pool

A Maisy Story Book Lucy Cousins

Maisy Makes Lemonade

A Maisy Story Book Lucy Cousins

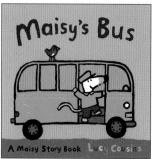

Maisy's Bus

A Maisy Story Book Lucy Cousins

Maisy Tidies Up

A Maisy Story Book Lucy Cousins

Maisy Makes Gingerbread

A Maisy Story Book Lucy Cousins

Maisy's Bathtime

A Maisy Story Book Lucy Cousins

My friend Maisy

Doctor Maisy

A Maisy Story Book Lucy Cousins

Maisy Goes Shopping

A Maisy Story Book Lucy Cousins

Available from all good booksellers

It's more fun with Maisy!